CELEBRATING THE FAMILY NAME OF KHAN

Celebrating the Family Name of Khan

Walter the Educator

Silent King Books
a WhichHead Entertainment Imprint

Copyright © 2024 by Walter the Educator

All rights reserved. No part of this book may be reproduced in any manner whatsoever without written permission except in the case of brief quotations embodied in critical articles and reviews.

First Printing, 2024

Disclaimer

This book is a literary work; the story is not about specific persons, locations, situations, and/or circumstances unless mentioned in a historical context. Any resemblance to real persons, locations, situations, and/or circumstances is coincidental. This book is for entertainment and informational purposes only. The author and publisher offer this information without warranties expressed or implied. No matter the grounds, neither the author nor the publisher will be accountable for any losses, injuries, or other damages caused by the reader's use of this book. The use of this book acknowledges an understanding and acceptance of this disclaimer.

Celebrating the Family Name of Khan is a memory book that belongs to the Celebrating Family Name Book Series by Walter the Educator. Collect them all and more books at WaltertheEducator.com

USE THE EXTRA SPACE TO DOCUMENT YOUR FAMILY MEMORIES THROUGHOUT THE YEARS

KHAN

Khan, a name of power and pride,

With roots that stretch both far and wide.

From ancient steppes to modern lore,

It echoes strength forevermore.

Through windswept plains and battles won,

The name Khan rises like the sun.

A heritage bold, unbowed, and free,

A legacy carved in history.

Beneath the stars of endless skies,

The Khan name shines, it never dies.

A spirit fierce, yet calm and wise,

With vision vast, it always flies.

In tales of honor, in songs of yore,

The name of Khan stands at the core.

A leader's heart, a warrior's will,

A name that time can never still.

Like rivers rushing, strong and deep,

The name of Khan its course will keep.

Through every challenge, every test,

It rises bold, it gives its best.

From noble courts to humble lands,

The Khan name weaves through shifting sands.

With unity, its strength unfolds,

A story that the future holds.

The Khan name builds where dreams are laid,

With courage vast and unafraid.

A guiding star through storm and night,

A beacon bright, a source of light.

In every voice, in every creed,

The name Khan grows, a mighty seed.

Through generations, strong and true,

It holds the promise of what's new.

With wisdom earned and battles past,

The Khan name's legacy will last.

It whispers tales of hope and grace,

Of those who shaped a timeless space.

So here's to Khan, a name of might,

A symbol bold, a shining light.

A family proud, a story grand,

Forever strong across the land.

ABOUT THE CREATOR

Walter the Educator is one of the pseudonyms for Walter Anderson. Formally educated in Chemistry, Business, and Education, he is an educator, an author, a diverse entrepreneur, and he is the son of a disabled war veteran. "Walter the Educator" shares his time between educating and creating. He holds interests and owns several creative projects that entertain, enlighten, enhance, and educate, hoping to inspire and motivate you. Follow, find new works, and stay up to date with Walter the Educator™ at WaltertheEducator.com

www.ingramcontent.com/pod-product-compliance
Lightning Source LLC
LaVergne TN
LVHW012051070526
838201LV00082B/3912